YOUR KNOWLEDGE HAS VALUE

- We will publish your bachelor's and master's thesis, essays and papers

- Your own eBook and book - sold worldwide in all relevant shops

- Earn money with each sale

Upload your text at www.GRIN.com and publish for free

Dilip Kumar

Testing the dynamics in the irregular fluctuations in the stock price changes of Indian stock market

GRIN Verlag

Bibliografische Information der Deutschen Nationalbibliothek:

Die Deutsche Bibliothek verzeichnet diese Publikation in der Deutschen National-bibliografie; detaillierte bibliografische Daten sind im Internet über http://dnb.d-nb.de/ abrufbar.

Imprint:

Copyright © 2013 GRIN Verlag GmbH
Druck und Bindung: Books on Demand GmbH, Norderstedt Germany
ISBN: 978-3-656-51459-6

This book at GRIN:

http://www.grin.com/en/e-book/262366/testing-the-dynamics-in-the-irregular-fluctuations-in-the-stock-price-changes

Testing the dynamics in the irregular fluctuations in the stock price changes of Indian stock market

Dilip Kumar
IFMR, Chennai, India.

Table of Contents

List of Tables

List of Figures

ABSTRACT

Stock price changes generally fluctuate stochastically. The purpose of this paper is to investigate whether the stochastic fluctuations in the stock price changes are random or have some kind of dynamics in the context of Indian stock market using a recently developed method, a small shuffle surrogate method, on daily data of six indices of National Stock Exchange of India Ltd (S&P CNX Nifty, CNX 100, S&P CNX 500, CNX Nifty Junior, CNX Midcap, CNX Smallcap). The study of dynamics in irregular fluctuations of asset price changes has implications related to risk management, asset allocation and trading strategies. A small shuffle surrogate method does not depend on any specific data distribution. Our findings support the presence of dynamics in the stock price changes of S&P CNX 500, CNX Nifty Junior, CNX Midcap and CNX Smallcap. On the other hand, price changes in S&P CNX Nifty and CNX 100 exhibit random behaviour. To test the robustness of the results, we also compute the variance ratio of the stock price changes over different asset holding periods. The result from the variance ratio test also supports the findings of small-shuffle surrogate analysis for all indices.

Keywords: Market efficiency, Small-shuffle surrogate method, Irregular fluctuations, Financial data,

1. Introduction

Stock price data shows irregular fluctuation, so it is important to investigate whether such irregular fluctuations in stock price changes are random or it has some kind of dynamics. Testing random behavior of financial time series helps in answering whether financial asset prices are predictable or not. This forms the base for testing weak form efficiency i.e. inability to forecast the asset prices using historical prices in the financial markets (Fama (1970)). The analysis of random walk in asset prices is important for practitioner as its presence can impact the implications related to risk management, portfolio selection and trading strategies. For financial market professionals, a correct assessment of the market is important to implement optimal investment and trading strategies. The foundation of literature of random walk hypothesis lies in the ground-breaking works of Bachelier (1900), Cootner (1964), Samuelson (1965) and Fama (1970).The basic assumption in testing random walk hypothesis (RWH) is the increments in asset prices to be IID (identically and independently distributed). If random walk hypothesis holds, then asset returns are non-predictable and market participants cannot make abnormal returns over their holding periods. The methods that test the IID disturbances are restrictive in nature. Testing random behavior of stock price changes has a long history. Earlier studies (pre – 1980) to test random walk hypothesis were inspired by the theories related to movements in the financial markets to the business cycle. Samuelson (1965) document that in efficient markets, price changes must be unpredictable which supports the statistical evidences provided by Kendall (1953), Cowles (1960), Osborne (1959 & 1962). The post – 1980 studies are inspired by the ground-breaking studies of Poterba and Summers (1988), Fama and French (1988) and Lo and MacKinlay (1988).

The central aim of this paper is to investigate whether the irregular fluctuations in the stock price changes in the stock indices from Indian stock market are random or have some kind of

2

dynamics. This paper attempts to answer a question: Is Indian stock market efficient and fair game? This paper uses a recently developed method, the small shuffle surrogate method (Nakamura and Small, 2005) to test the null hypothesis that price changes are independently distributed. We also make use of Lo and MacKinlay's (1988) variance ratio test to confirm the findings obtained by small-shuffle surrogate method.

The remainder of this paper is organized as follows: Section 2 discusses the literature review on the issue. Section 3 introduces the methodology used in this study. Section 4 discusses the data and computational details. Section 5 reports the empirical results. Section 6 highlights the limitation of the study and future research and section 7 concludes with summary and main findings.

2. Review of Literature/Theatrical Background of the Study

The literature of random walk in stock prices has a long history and is still a prominent topic of research in finance (Kendall (1953), Fama (1965, 1970), De Bondt and Thaler (1985) and Bollerslev and Hodrick (1992)). If random walk model holds then prediction by analysts is like that of astrologer. Traditional random walk tests[1] of asset returns were primarily based on serial correlation of price changes. Several methods have been developed to test whether the data is independently distributed or not. The most popular methods involve estimation of variance ratio statistics and Hurst exponents. Hurst exponent is a popular way of detecting random walk in a process. The pioneering work by Lo and MacKinlay (1988) provide a robust way of identification of random walk in the time series by mean of variance ratio test. Chow and Denning (1993) apply the multiple comparison statistical approach on Lo and MacKinlay (1988) methodology to estimate multiple variance ratio statistics which become the basis of other multiple variance ratio tests.

---

[1] Based on studies before 1980s

3

Nakamura and Small (2005) propose a small-shuffle surrogate method to examine the dynamics in the stochastic data. Nakamura and Small (2006) investigate whether the irregular fluctuations in daily gold prices and daily Japanese Yen/US dollar exchange rates are random or have some kind of dynamics by applying the small-shuffle surrogate method and find that these data are not random but exhibit some kind of dynamics. Nakamura and Small (2007a, 2007b) test the random walk hypothesis in stock market, exchange rates and commodity market and find results in support of random behavior of these data. Nakamura and Small (2007c) investigate whether there are correlation structures in short-term variabilities in US stock prices and exchange rates from the viewpoint of deterministic dynamical systems using small shuffle surrogate method and find that the data are not independent.

3. Research Methodology and Research Hypothesis

3.1 The Random walk Hypothesis

According to random walk model, tomorrow's price is expected to be the same as today's price. Suppose $x(t)$ be the original data, so for x(t) to follow random walk,

$$E_t\big(x(t)/\Omega(t-1)\big) = x(t-1) \qquad (1)$$

Where $\Omega(t-1)$ be the information set consist of information upto time t – 1 which also includes $x(t-1)$. In other words, random walk model implies that $x(t) - x(t-1)$ is a fair game, that is,

$$E_t\big((x(t) - x(t-1))/\Omega(t-1)\,\big) = 0 \qquad (2)$$

The random walk model can also be written as:

$$x(t) = x(t-1) + \varepsilon(t) \qquad (3)$$

Where $\varepsilon(t)$ is the disturbance term and usually considered to be IID (identically and independently distributed) noise. Here, the coefficient of $x(t-1)$ is explicitly one. Hence, from (3), the value of random walk is integrated by the noise term $\varepsilon(t)$. Random walk is a

4

stochastic process which does not depend on the history of the data. If random walk hypothesis holds, then asset returns are non-predictable and market participants cannot make abnormal returns over their holding periods.

Null hypothesis that we want to test in this paper is:

$$H_0 = \Delta x(t) \text{ is independently distributed} \tag{4}$$

The alternative hypothesis against the Null hypothesis is:

$$H_1 = \Delta x(t) \text{ is not independently distributed} \tag{5}$$

3.2 Small-shuffle surrogate method

Nakamura and Small (2005) propose a method, called small-shuffle surrogate method, to investigate whether the temporal correlations in the data is absent or data is independently distributed random variables. The small-shuffle surrogate method addresses the null hypothesis (equation 4) that the irregular fluctuations are independently distributed random variables, that is, there is no short term dynamics or determinism in the data. The small-shuffle surrogate method does not depend on the data distribution.

Suppose $x(t)$ be the log of stock price and $i(t)$ be the index of $x(t)$, that is, $i(t) = t$, so $x(i(t)) = x(t)$. Suppose g(t) be Gaussian random number. Hence, the procedure for generating small-shuffle surrogate data is given as follow:

1. First find $i'(t) = i(t) + Ag(t)$, where A is an amplitude. Nakamura and Small (2006) find that A = 1 is adequate for financial market data.

2. Sort $i'(t)$ by the rank-order and let the index of $i'(t)$ be $\hat{\imath}(t)$ (rank-order the perturbed index).

3. Obtain the surrogate data, $s(t) = x(\hat{\imath}(t))$, that is, reorder the original data with the perturbed index.

In the small shuffle surrogate method, the data is shuffled on the small scale. This destroys the local structure in the short term variability (irregular fluctuations) of the data but preserve

5

the global behavior (trends) of the data. Hence, the shuffled data has the same probability distribution as that of original data (Nakamura and Small (2006)).

We have applied small-shuffle surrogate method on logarithm of stock price and to the returns to test the consistency of data with random walk. Since, random walk shows irregular fluctuations and also exhibit dynamics. This refers the fact that the stochastic nature of data should have dynamics. If we find that the stochastic nature of data has dynamics, then there is possibility that the original data is random walk. If data is random walk, then the first difference data should be independently distributed (time-varying) random variables.

We have used auto-correlation (AC) function and average mutual information (AMI) as two discriminating statistics for hypothesis testing (Nakamura and Small (2006)). Auto-correlation (AC) function helps to examine the linear correlation in data and average mutual information (AMI) is an estimate of non-linear correlation in data. These statistics can answer the question: on average, how much does one learn about the future from the past (Abarbanel (1996))?

To examine whether the null hypothesis is rejected, we use Monte Carlo hypothesis testing technique in which we inspect whether the discriminating statistics of original data lie within or outside the statistical distribution of surrogate data (Theiler and Prichard (1996)). If the estimated discriminating statistics of original data fall within the distribution of surrogate data, we can say that the null hypothesis cannot be rejected. In this paper, we have generated 99 small-shuffle surrogate data to test the null hypothesis. Nakamura and Small (2006) find that the multiple comparison problems are common in surrogate data, so they recommend using AC and AMI as complementary statistics. Nakamura and Small (2005) find that AC and AMI test statistics are meaningful only for small lags, because these discriminating test statistics for surrogate data and original data coincide at larger lags.

6

3.3 Variance ratio test

The variance ratio test exploits the property that, if a series of asset returns is purely random, then the variance of k-period return (k-period differences of x(t)) is k times the variance of a one-period return. The variance ratio with k holding periods is defined as:

$$VR(y:k) = \left\{ \frac{1}{Tk} \sum_{t=k}^{T} (y(t) + y(t-1) + .. + y(t-k+1) - k\hat{\mu})^2 \right\} \div \left\{ \frac{1}{T} \sum_{t=1}^{T} (y(t) - \hat{\mu})^2 \right\} (6)$$

where y(t) = Δx(t) and $\hat{\mu} = T^{-1} \sum_{t=1}^{T} y(t)$.

For data showing conditional heteroskedasticity, Lo and MacKinlay (1988) proposed the heteroskedasticity test statistic *M(y;k)*

$$M(y:k) = (VR(y:k) - 1) \left(\sum_{j=1}^{k-1} \left[\frac{2(k-j)}{k} \right]^2 \delta_j \right)^{-\frac{1}{2}} \tag{7}$$

which follows the standard normal distribution asymptotically under the null hypothesis that *V(k)* = 1, where

$$\delta_j = \left\{ \sum_{t=j+1}^{T} (y(t) - \hat{\mu})^2 (y(t-j) - \hat{\mu})^2 \right\} \div \left\{ \left[\sum_{t=1}^{T} (y(t) - \hat{\mu})^2 \right]^2 \right\}$$

4. Data and computational details

In order to test the random behavior of stock prices in Indian stock market, we have used daily observations of six indices of National Stock Exchange of India Ltd. The indices[2] used in this paper are S&P CNX Nifty (most commonly used index, composed of 50 firms from 24 sectors), CNX100 (composed of 100 firms from 38 sectors), S&P CNX 500 (first broad based benchmark of Indian capital market), CNX Nifty Junior (composed of next 50 liquid stocks

---

[2] The indices used in this paper use free float market capitalization methodology.

after S&P CNX Nifty), CNX Midcap (capture the movement in the midcap segment of the market), CNX Smallcap Index (reflects the movement in small capitalized segment of the financial market) covering all the major segments of the Indian market. All data are obtained from www.nseindia.com. The period of study for S&P CNX Nifty is from 3 May 1994 to 29 April 2011 (4214 observations); for CNX100 is from 2 Jan 2003 to 29 April 2011 (2077 observations); for S&P CNX 500 is from 8 June 1999 to 29 April 2011 (2971 observations); for CNX Nifty Junior is from 5 Oct 1995 to 29 April 2011 (3887 observations); for CNX Midcap is from 2 Jan 2001 to 29 April 2011 (2577 observations) and for CNX Smallcap Index is from 2 Jan 2004 to 29 April 2011 (1824 observations). We have used the following abbreviations for the indices in this paper, that is Nifty for S&P CNX Nifty, CNX100 for CNX 100, CNX500 for S&P CNX 500, JUR for CNX Nifty Junior, MID for CNX Midcap 50, SMA for CNX Smallcap index.

Table 1: Descriptive Statistics of Stock Returns

	NIFTY	CNX100	CNX500	JUR	MID	SMA
Mean	0.000	0.001	0.001	0.001	0.001	0.001
Median	0.001	0.002	0.002	0.001	0.003	0.003
Stdev	0.017	0.017	0.017	0.019	0.016	0.017
Min	-0.131	-0.130	-0.129	-0.131	-0.129	-0.129
Max	0.163	0.159	0.150	0.138	0.115	0.089
Quartile 1	-0.008	-0.007	-0.007	-0.008	-0.006	-0.006
Quartile 3	0.009	0.010	0.009	0.011	0.009	0.010
Skewness	$-0.150^{\#}$	$-0.369^{\#}$	$-0.499^{\#}$	$-0.506^{\#}$	$-0.948^{\#}$	$-1.203^{\#}$
Kurtosis	$6.367^{\#}$	$8.343^{\#}$	$6.122^{\#}$	$4.554^{\#}$	$6.977^{\#}$	$7.178^{\#}$
Jarque-Bera	$7144.34^{\#}$	$6086.45^{\#}$	$4772.52^{\#}$	$3530.65^{\#}$	$5625.23^{\#}$	$4368.99^{\#}$
Shapiro-Wilk	$0.947^{\#}$	$0.923^{\#}$	$0.935^{\#}$	$0.943^{\#}$	$0.916^{\#}$	$0.899^{\#}$
ARCH LM	$353.257^{\#}$	$228.298^{\#}$	$376.004^{\#}$	$609.204^{\#}$	$482.888^{\#}$	$422.055^{\#}$
N	4214	2077	2971	3887	2577	1824

$^{\#}$ Means significant at 1% level of significance.

Table 1 reports the descriptive statistics of all sample returns. The median daily returns for CNX Midcap and CNX Smallcap are the highest of all indices. S&P CNX Nifty shows lowest mean daily return with respect to other indices[3]. CNX Nifty junior seems to be more volatile than other indices. All indices returns are showing significant negative skewness and excess kurtosis. Jarque-Bera and Shapiro-Wilk tests strongly reject the normality of the returns. ARCH-LM test supports the presence of conditional heteroskedasticity in the returns series.

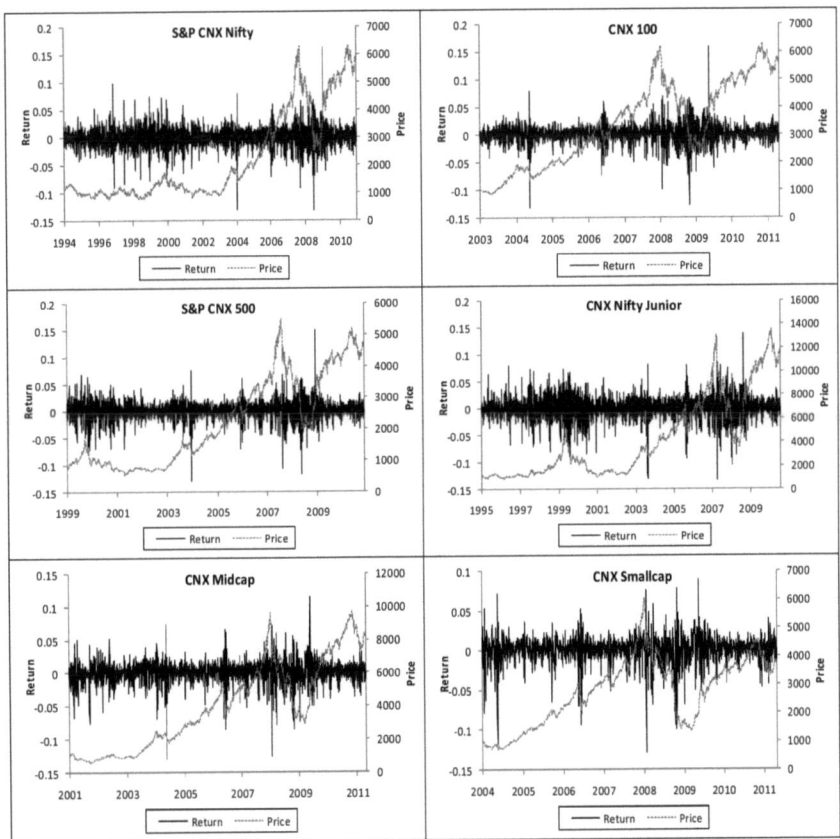

Figure 1: Time plots for returns and prices data series for all the indices.

[3] Returns for other indices are nearly same.

9

Figure 1 presents the time plots of returns and prices data series of all the indices respectively. The primary vertical axis represents return and secondary vertical axis represents price. We can observe larger volatility during the period of dot-com bubble (1998 to 2003) and sub-prime crisis (2008).

5. Empirical Results

We apply small-shuffle surrogate method on log of stock prices and on returns (log-differenced prices) to examine the martingale behavior of stock prices. Figure 2 presents the plots of auto-correlation function (AC) (first column) and average mutual information (AMI) (second column) as a function of time lags for log of stock prices for all the indices used in this study. These plots show the difference between the AC and the AMI of original data and the distribution of small-shuffle surrogate data. The difference between the auto-correlation (AC) function of original log of stock prices and the distribution of small-shuffle surrogate data is negligibly small for CNX 100, CNX Midcap and CNX Smallcap indices. Also, for S&P CNX Nifty, S&P CNX 500 and CNX Nifty Junior, the AC of original log of prices fall outside the distributions of small-shuffle surrogate data. The AMI of original log of prices for all the indices falls outside the distribution of small-shuffle surrogate. This supports the evidence that the irregular fluctuations in log of stock prices of all indices have some kind of dynamics. At this stage, these results support the fact that there is a possibility that the indices data are random walk.

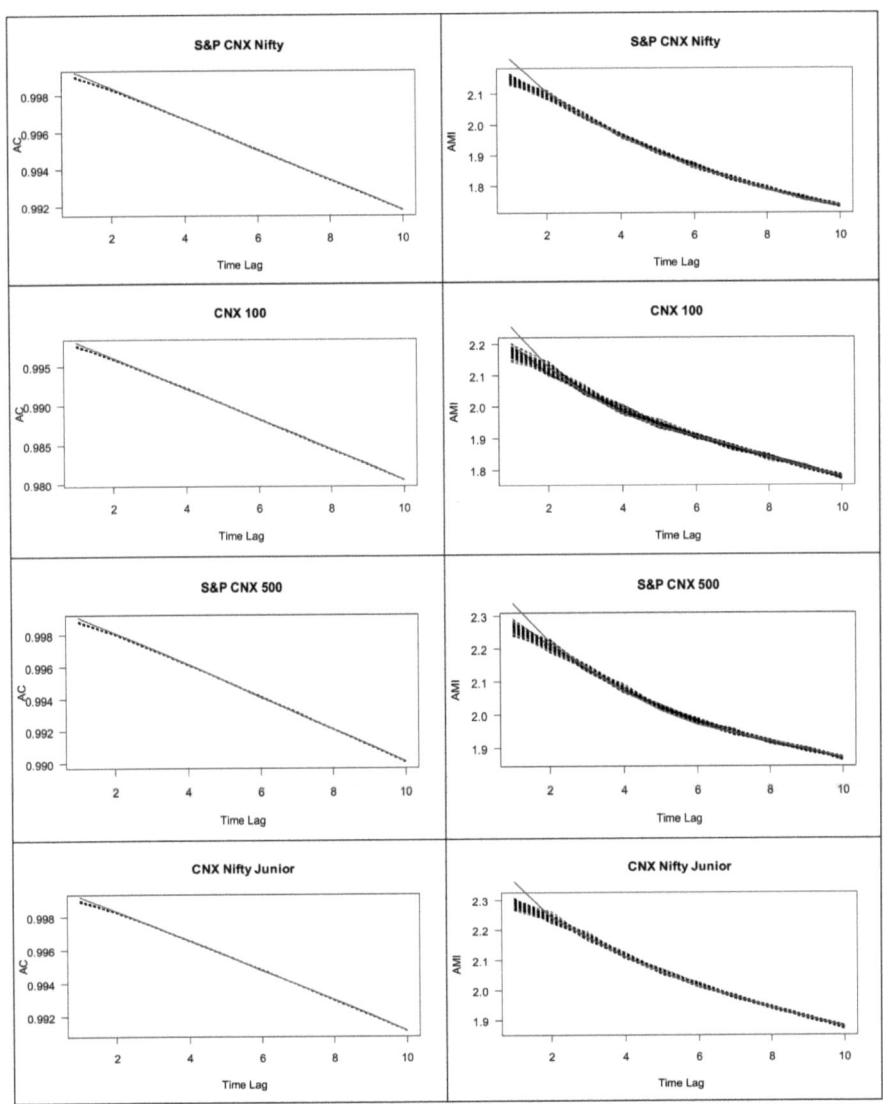

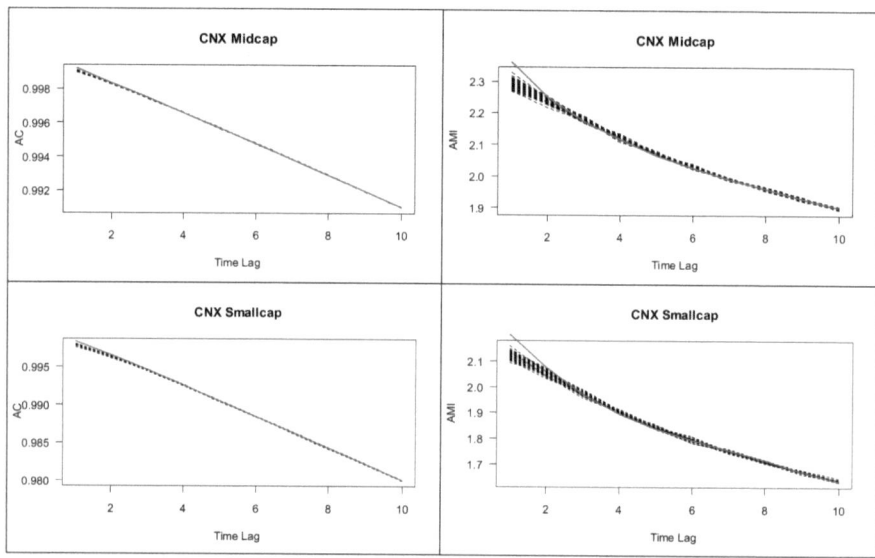

Figure 2: Plot for AC and AMI of log of prices for all indices. The solid line is the original data and dotted lines are the small-shuffle surrogate data.

Now, we apply the small-shuffle surrogate method on the log differenced data for all indices. Figure 3 presents the plots of auto-correlation function (AC) (first column) and average mutual information (AMI) (second column) for log difference prices for all indices under study. The AC and AMI of original log-differenced data falls outside the distribution of small-shuffle surrogate data for S&P CNX 500, CNX Nifty Junior, CNX Midcap and CNX Smallcap. This helps us to conclude that the daily log of closing price data of S&P CNX 500, CNX Nifty Junior, CNX Midcap and CNX Smallcap are violating the null hypothesis of independently distributed random variables (random walk). On the flip side, we do not find any evidence against the rejection of null hypothesis for S&P CNX Nifty and CNX 100.

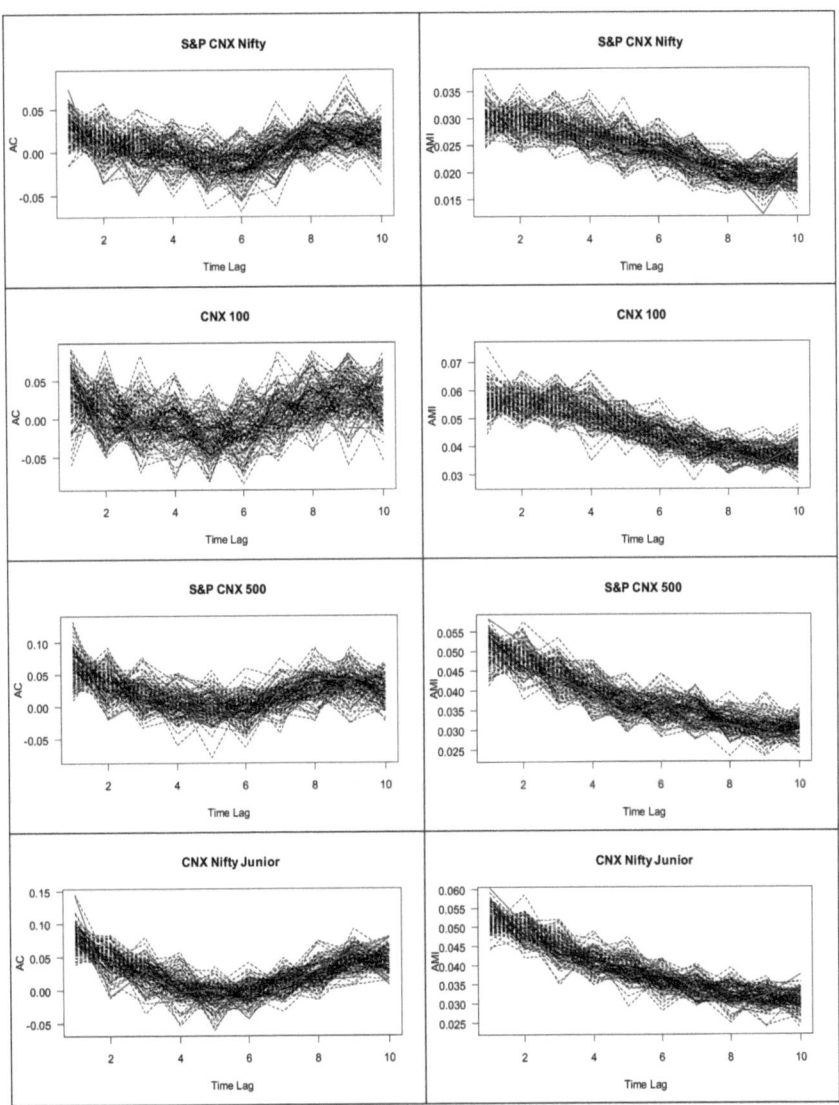

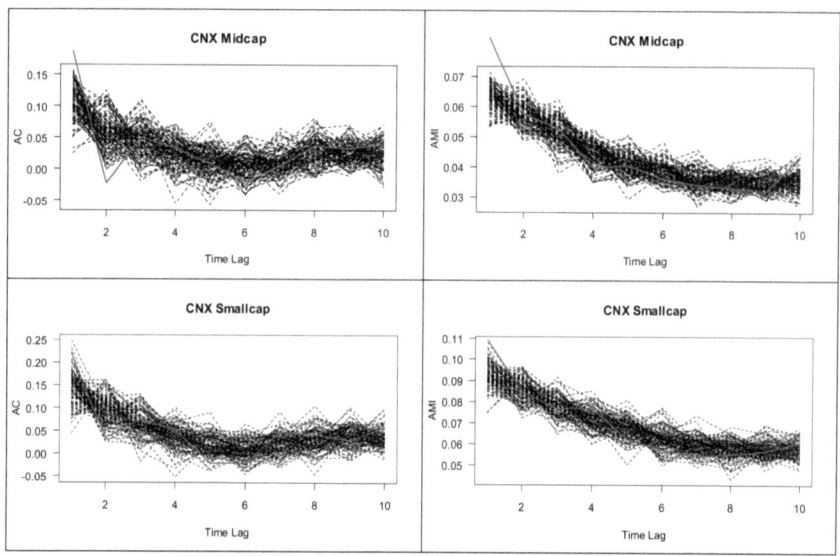

Figure 3: **Plot for AC and AMI of log differenced prices for all indices. The solid line is the original data and dotted lines are the small-shuffle surrogate data.**

To test the robustness of the results obtained by small-shuffle surrogate analysis, we apply variance ratio test. Figure 4 presents the plots of variance ratio with 95% confidence band for different holding periods in days (up to 52 days) for all the indices under study. Variance ratios for S&P CNX Nifty and CNX 100 are outside the band only for some initial periods (upto 6 days holding period for S&P CNX Nifty and 4 days holding period for CNX 100) and remain within the 95% confidence band for all other periods which provides little evidence of violation of null hypothesis. On the other hand, the variance ratios for S&P CNX 500, CNX Nifty Junior, CNX Midcap and CNX Smallcap are outside the 95% confidence band for all holding periods and in particular, provide support for the presence of momentum for longer holding periods also.

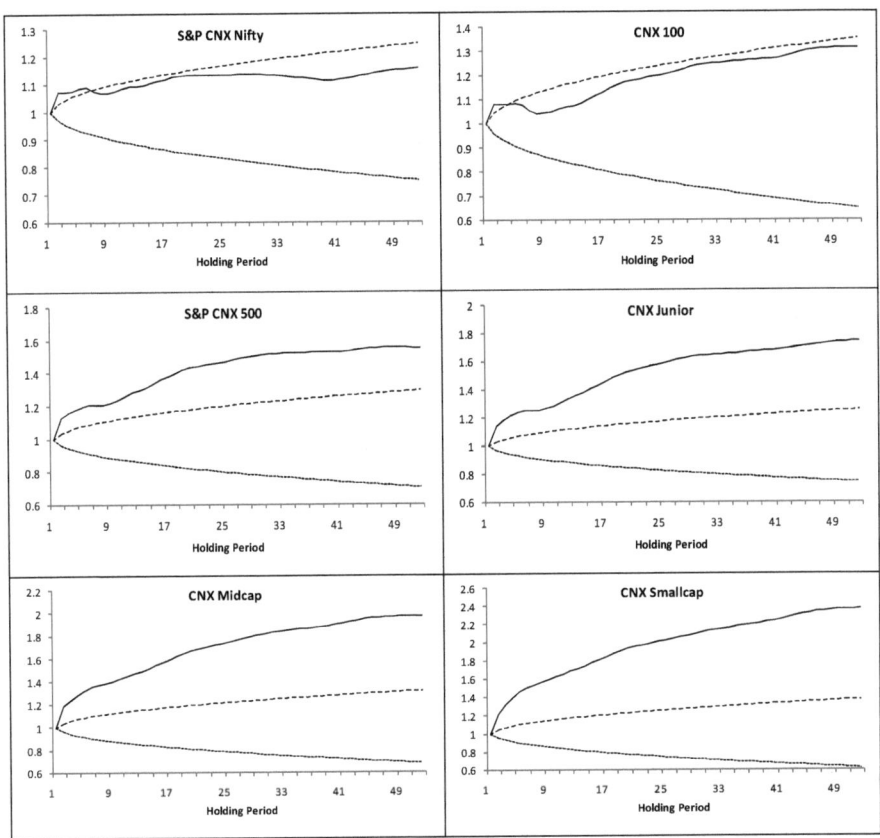

Figure 4: Plot for variance ratios with 95% confidence band for all indices. The solid line represents the variance ratio and dashed and dotted lines represent upper and lower 95% confidence band respectively.

6. Limitation of the study and future research

The present study investigates the dynamics in the irregular fluctuation of daily stock price changes. Further research can be undertaken to investigate the dynamics in the high frequency stock price data (tick by tick price changes).

15

7. Conclusion

This paper utilizes the recently developed small-shuffle surrogate method to investigate whether the irregular fluctuations in the stock price changes have some kind of dynamics or not for six indices, which cover major part of Indian stock market. This method does not depend on the specific data distribution. Our results provide evidence that the daily data of S&P CNX 500, CNX Nifty Junior, CNX Midcap and CNX Smallcap are violating the null hypothesis of independently distributed random variables (random walk) which support the presence of dynamics in the irregular fluctuations of daily stock prices. We also test the validity of the results by the use of variance ratio test which help us to conclude that except S&P CNX Nifty and CNX 100, all other indices reject the null hypothesis of change in stock prices to be independently distributed.

References

Abarbanel, H. D. I. (1996). Analysis of observed chaotic data. Springer, New York.

Bachelier, L. (1900). 'Theorie de la speculation' (PhD thesis in mathematics). Annal Sci Ecole Norm Superieure (1900), Vol. 17, pp. 21 – 86.

Bollerslev T. and R. Hodrick (1992). Financial Market Efficiency Tests. NBER Working Paper Series, Working paper no. 4108

Bondt W. and R. Thaler (1985). Does the Stock Market Overreact? The Journal of Finance, Vol. 40 No. 3, pp. 793-805.

Chow, V. and K. Denning (1993). A Simple Variance Ratio Test. Journal of Econometrics, Vol. 58, pp. 385 – 401.

Cootner, P. H. (1964). The random character of stock market prices. Cambridge, MA: MIT Press (1964).

Cowles, A. (1960). A revision of previous conclusions regarding stock price behavior. Econometrica, Vol. 28, pp. 909 - 915.

Fama, E. (1965). The Behavior of Stock-Market Prices. The Journal of Business, Vol. 38 No. 1, pp. 34-105.

Fama, E. (1965). Random Walks in Stock Market Prices. Financial Analysts Journal, Vol. 21 No. 5, pp. 55-59.

Fama, E. (1970). Efficient Capital Markets: A Review of Theory and Empirical Work. The Journal of Finance, Vol. 25 No. 2, pp. 383-417

Fama, E. and K. French (1988). Permanent and Temporary Components of Stock Prices. The Journal of Political Economy, Vol. 96 No. 2, pp. 246-273.

Kendall, M. (1953). The analysis of economic time series - part 1: Prices. Journal of the Royal Statistical Society, Vol. 96, pp. 11 - 25.

Lo, A. and A. C. MacKinlay (1988). Stock market prices do not follow random walks: Evidence from a simple specification test, The Review of Financial Studies, Vol. 1, pp. 41-66.

Nakamura, T. and M. Small (2005). Small-shuffle surrogate data: testing for dynamics in fluctuating data with trends. Physical Review E, Vol. 72, pp. 056216-1 – 056216-6.

Nakamura, T. and M. Small (2006). Testing for dynamics in the irregular fluctuations of financial data. Physica A, Vol. 366, pp. 377 – 386.

Nakamura, T. and M. Small (2007a). Tests of the random walk hypothesis for financial data. Physica A, Vol. 377, pp. 599 – 615.

Nakamura, T. and M. Small (2007b). Testing random walk. Physics Letters A, Vol. 362, pp. 189–197.

Nakamura, T. and M. Small (2007c). Correlation structures in short-term variabilities of stock indices and exchange rates. Physica A, Vol. 383, pp. 96–101.

Osborne, M. (1959). Brownian motion in the stock market. Operations Research, Vol. 7, pp. 145 - 173.

Osborne, M. (1962). Periodic structures in the brownian motion of stock prices. Operations Research, Vol. 10, pp. 345 - 379.

Potreba, J. M. and L. H. Summers (1988). Mean reversion in stock returns: evidence and implications. Journal of Financial Economics, Vol. 22, pp. 27 – 59.

Samuelson, P. (1965). Proof that properly anticipated prices fluctuate randomly. Industrial Management Review, Spring, Vol. 6, pp. 41-49.

Theiler, J. and D. Prichard (1996). Constrained-realization Monte Carlo method for hypothesis testing. Physica D, Vol. 94, Vol. 221-235.